Be Blessed,
Libby Dalton

LIBBY'S CHRISTMAS LETTERS

Libby Dalton

ISBN: 979-8-9854044-8-7 (Paperback)
ISBN: 979-8-9854044-9-4 (Hardcover)
ISBN: 979-8-9854044-7-0 (eBook)

With Foreword &
Devotional Thoughts

by Roy Lessin

GRATEFUL for Charles, my husband, who has encouraged me every year to follow through with my Christmas letter. He has always believed in me and has walked through this amazing journey with me, holding me up when I doubted myself.

GRATEFUL for Denise McCormick and Debba Smith who helped each year to put my letter together, always choosing just the right paper and retyping to make sure my letter looked just perfect. They were always excited each year when I would say that my letter was ready.

GRATEFUL for Linda Knorr who has shared my letters, knocked on every door possible, and has never given up with the vision for my letters.

GRATEFUL for Darian Byrd who spent hours compiling all the original letters into a single document. My heart is full.

GRATEFUL that Linda introduced me to Roy Lessin.

GRATEFUL for "Because of Jesus, Today Is Your Best Day," by Roy Lessin. Since 2007, Linda, myself, and now many others have placed this devotion book in the hands of thousands of people.

GRATEFUL for ROY LESSIN who is the most humble person I have ever met. To work with him through this entire process and then to have him write the Introduction add scripture to each story, ONLY God could have provided this.

GRATEFUL for those God Nudges.

GRATEFUL that YOU are reading this.

GRATEFUL that truly today is my best day... because of Jesus.

Table of Contents

Foreword

by Roy Lessin

Libby's Letters is a collection of Christmas letters sent to her family and friends from 2007-2021. Her letters are not filled with family news, but good news. Each one tells an amazing story that reveals God's caring ways as He seeks to draw others to Himself.

My first Libby Letter arrived in my mailbox in early December of 2020. With it came a personal note from Libby that began with these words: "I feel so much like I know you. You have been such a big part of my life."

I first heard the name Libby Dalton through Linda Knorr. The two women were close friends living in Greenville, South Carolina. In 2007 Linda's husband, Jim, was diagnosed with AML leukemia and given a short time to live. To encourage Linda and Jim, Libby brought them some homemade muffins, a copy of my book *Because of Jesus, Today Is Your Best Day*, and a note that said,

This little book is for you to read to Jim each day.

Linda took Libby's note to heart and began reading daily with Jim. The following quote is from Linda as she experienced her last day together with Jim:

We were reading the book straight through for the sixth time when on December 23, 2007, Jim and I enjoyed coffee and read this together, "Today is your best day because of forever." 'Forever' was a profound word because on that day we experienced God's promise "today is your best day because of heaven."

At the time of Jim's passing, Libby and Linda were strangers to me. We had never met, never spoken to each other, and never corresponded. That all changed when I was contacted by David Thomas, a state senator in South Carolina. He was a friend of Linda's. He told me about her loss and how God had used *Because of Jesus, Today Is Your Best Day* in the lives of Linda and Jim. He asked me if I would consider contacting Linda directly to encourage her and included her email address.

A few months passed before I contacted Linda and she got back to me. It was during that time I learned the details of Linda's story and heard about her friend Libby gifting her with my book. I was so overjoyed by what Linda shared that I asked her to write an introduction to my book when it was reprinted.

For the next twelve years, the only thing I knew personally about Libby's life was that she was a great baker who made the world's best muffins, and then her 2007–2021 Christmas letters arrived!

I took my time going through the collection, slowly reading and reflecting upon one Christmas letter a day. When I completed the letters, I sent off this note to a friend: "I've never read anything quite like them. They grabbed my heart, brought tears to my eyes, and left me in awe of God's ways. If you're looking for anointed God stories, you need to read them."

Through Libby's letters, I learned more about her heart. I saw her life is an adventure of faith, making herself available for God to use in the common, routine, and ordinary things in her day. In answer to her prayers, the Holy Spirit guided her steps to reach those who are often ignored, used her voice to speak to those who might not want to listen, and strengthened her hands to help those who didn't know where to turn.

I hope you will be delighted reading Libby's Letters. May they warm your heart with a smile, a tear, and a little nudge to take the next step of obedience that will result in your own amazing God story.

Roy Lessin

Just a Bar of Soap, Lord
(Christmas 2007)

At the heart of Christmas,
This one thing we know—
Jesus came to save us,
And wash us white as snow.

Wash me, and I will be whiter than snow.
Psalm 51:7

Devotional Thought

~ Roy Lessin

I had taken the day off to work on our Christmas tree. I was making ornaments out of curtain rings (gold ones), and I was so smart. I was cross-stitching a scene to go in each one. Oh, how beautiful they were. I was carefully working and then gluing them onto the rings. The phone rang.

"What time are we meeting? Oh, how I love our Friday lunches together. Where are we going?" It was my mother, and in all my excitement, I had forgotten it was Friday. Well, I said, "Let's have lunch here today. I am preparing something special, and I thought it would be fun." "I will be there at 12:00, and just look forward to our time together. I love you," she said as she hung up. Great, now get busy, put down the decorations, and prepare this wonderful lunch in the next hour. As I began, I thought about one of mother's favorites, my quiche, and I immediately began preparing a feast that even I, myself, am amazed with.

When mother arrived, I had my ornaments out to show her just what I was doing.

"How beautiful," she began. "Would you make one for each lady in my Sunday school class? They would love them. I will buy the materials if you will make them." I could not believe what I was hearing. "Whoa, are you kidding? I will never get through if I take on that project," I informed her. "Oh, that is fine darling. I know how busy you are," was her reply.

After a great lunch (which I had prepared), she left and I walked out to the mailbox. There in my mailbox was a little devotion book that my mother had mailed to me entitled *Mini Devotions for the Busy Mother*, with a note that said "Just thinking of you, I love you, Mom." I opened the book, and the first story was about a lonely woman in a nursing home just asking, as she was washing her hands, "Lord, if you would just send me a bar of soap for Christmas."

I ran back into the house and began my project. By Saturday evening, I had finished all of the ornaments and knew what Sunday would bring. I got up Sunday morning and headed to my mom's church. I found her Sunday school class and, to her surprise, handed her the ornaments to give to each member in her class. How excited they were. How excited she was. How truly proud she was of her daughter at that moment.

Just a bar of soap, Lord. Just a small gift that made such a difference. These ornaments were my bars of soap. When my mother died, the ladies in her Sunday school class came to visit, and pinned on their garments were those ornaments. They never went on a Christmas tree. They wore them each and every Christmas.

This Christmas, may each of you be used by Him to cheer someone. Believe me, if you will allow God to direct you in blessing others, *you* will receive *great* blessings. Merry Christmas, and please know of the love expressed in this message for each of you and for our Savior,

Charles and Libby
(Luke 6:38a)

Update from Libby

My mother was the perfect mother. She worked at a time when other mothers did not. She began her career with Southern Bell (now AT&T), and after years of service, she became the first woman serving in a management position. She never saw herself as a woman of importance. She always told me, "I just love Jesus, and He has provided my steps." One thing I will always remember, the men she worked with had such respect for her. Anytime she was at a breakfast or luncheon, she was always called on to say the blessing. I told her one time I thought that was amazing, and she said," not really." She went on to say that the first time she attended a breakfast with the group she sat, waiting on someone to say the blessing and when they did not say the blessing, she ask if it was alright if she did. Always, after that, she was assigned that honor.

Joy Comes When?
(Christmas 2008)

Jesus wants you to behold His glory for the pure joy of it. His glory is so great that it will take you an eternity to behold it—His glory will keep on delighting you, over and over again. It will be one continuous "Wow, Jesus, Wow!" forever and ever.

Now unto Him that is able to...present you faultless before the presence of His glory with exceeding joy.
Jude 1:24

Devotional Thought

~ Roy Lessin

For the past two years, I have chosen a word that would become my word for the entire year. This year, I chose the word "joy." As you read this, please keep that in mind.

We have moved. And we moved, and we moved, and we moved. The entire summer was spent relocating and renovating. One very, very hot July day, I decided that I would load up all of my Christmas decorations and move them to our new home. After several hours of unloading from the attic to the truck, I was ready. Now, our truck is a 1976 Truck that has not been remodeled. It is one of those trucks that when you put your blinker on, no one will let you in any lane; everyone wants to do their part to keep you off the road. But I love our truck.

I began my eleven-mile trip down interstate singing Christmas carols thinking this would help me not think about the 98-degree weather. After about five minutes, I happened to look out the back of the truck and saw a number of my gorgeous red bows had just blown off the truck. *(That is what I get for not waiting on Charles to pack things securely).* I pulled off of the road immediately and gathered up my bows and was quietly saying, "Thank you, Jesus, that I am safely on my way again."

When I arrived at our new home, a car pulled in behind me which I did not recognize. She got out of her beautiful, air-conditioned car, and in her hands, she had nine red bows. She said, "These blew off your truck, and for some reason, I just felt I had to stop and pick them up. I did not think I would catch up with you. I was afraid to blow the horn; I did not think you could be going that far" (*what she wanted to say was, "In that truck, you were not going very far"*).

I could not believe my eyes. Someone was nice enough to help me and had not stopped to think that what she was doing was just as crazy as what I was doing. I began to thank her over and over, and then I introduced myself. Then she said, "My name is *Joy*." Wow. Her name was *Joy*. I could not believe my ears. I just started crying right there. She did not know how to react. I began to tell her that my word for the year was "joy" and that I looked for *joy* in everything I did, and to actually have a real Joy standing in my driveway, wow, what a day. Then, she began to cry. I ask if I could help, and in one hour, I learned that she was a broken woman who was covered with cuts and bruises and was in the process of moving away from an abusive marriage. She had no idea why she had followed me home.

At that point, I knew *joy* does come in all sorts of packages. It comes with red ribbons all wrapped around it. It comes with a baby that was the greatest gift any of us could ever receive. It came in a woman who brought me great *joy* and a woman who left with *joy* in her heart. She began her new life in the driveway of our new home. She left with a small Christmas tree and some of my red bows. But more than that, she left with real *joy*. An old truck did not stop her. She left with a reminder that no one could rob her of her *joy*. I hope someday she returns to the upstate, but if she does not, we shared real *joy* and the *joy* of what each of us are sharing this season. Yes, Jesus is the reason for our *joy*.

Charles and Libby

Update from Libby

Why in the world would a woman stop on the side of the interstate and pick up Christmas bows? Why would she follow a beat-up ole truck? She was in a hurry to pick up her children, and they were headed out of town. She had no answers, but I did. When she pulled into our driveway, she honestly did not know what was about to happen. Here was a woman who had been severely beaten, bruises she had tried to cover with makeup pouring out her heart to a woman who was already sobbing. See, I wanted to have my pity party because it was so hot and I was so tired. Then, when she told me her name, I must have sounded like some crazy person telling her all about my word for the year and realizing that I was already feeling that God nudge. We talked and prayed together, and I told her she could have a better life for her and her two children. She left our new home to go and pick up her two children to head for their new home in another state. She had three little suitcases in the back. Would we ever see each other again? She could give me no information as to where she was going, but I did tell her we would see each other again one day. She ask me how I knew that, and I told her because of Heaven. I also reminded her to think on her special name "Joy." Jesus, others, and you, let that become her message to the world.

Joy to You
(Christmas 2009)

May you find Jesus to be
the peace for every uncertainty,
the supply for every need,
the release for every burden,
the comfort for every sorrow,
the joy for every day.

His name shall be called...Mighty God!
Isaiah 9:6

Devotional Thought

~ Roy Lessin

My word for 2009 is "faith." It was a tough decision to choose a word this year. I had settled on *faith* and then, in June, *joy* came back into my life.

It was another hot day. The doorbell rang, and it was *joy*. I was so thrilled to see her. I had so many questions for her. Was she safe? Were her children safe? Where was she living? Did she know I prayed for her each day? I allowed my mind to stop racing and realized I needed to be still and listen to her. In her arms she had bunches of red bows. She began by crying and saying she had found all this ribbon on sale after Christmas last year, and she bought it. This was her first major purchase on her own. She had never made a Christmas bow herself. She confessed that she had kept one of my bows she had gathered out of the road just to remember our time together.

As she looked at the bow she had saved, she began to think that maybe she could make bows.

As she began to copy the beautiful bow, she became more and more excited with what she was able to do. This was her story:

"I had never done anything like this," she said. "As I worked, I began to see that I truly could do this. The first day, I sat in the floor and made bows with all the ribbon I had purchased. I began to think, *God, this is a small talent, but I do have a talent.* That evening, I placed the bows throughout the tiny apartment that myself and two children were living in. At dinner that evening, I came to the dinner table with a bow tied around my neck, and my children laughed like I had never heard them laugh. That night, I went to bed praying my usual prayer to God thanking Him for safety for me and my children and thanking him for loving us and praying for a job. The very next morning, I knew what I was going to do. I delivered the children to school and headed to the grocery store just around the corner from our apartment. I talked with the manager about a job in their floral area. He said they had nothing, but his sister had a shop and hired people to help during busy seasons. Valentines was approaching, and he knew she was very busy. While I still had my nerve, I headed to her shop. I had to tell the truth: that I had no experience but I could make bows."

The next sentence out of Joy's mouth caused me to freeze, and I felt the chill bumps all over my body (*my Jesus bumps*).

Joy said, "The woman looked at me and said, 'For some reason, I am going to step out in *faith* and hire you.'" Wow, my word. I immediately stopped Joy's story and told her of my word this year. I told her how I had prayed for her every day and every day I ask for *faith* for her to move ahead, for *faith* in herself. "Faith" meant believing.

We talked for a long time, and Joy reassured me that she was finally safe but still could not tell me where they were living. She did say that she and the children were healing.

As Joy prepared to leave, I brought her into my kitchen and shared with her a verse I had placed over my sink. I somehow felt it would be a part of my Christmas letter, but how I did not know. The verse is "Faith is being sure of what you hope for and certain of what you do not see" (Hebrews 11:1).

My *faith* is in a little baby who every Christmas reminds me of the *hope* for me and people like Joy. With every Christmas bow you see this year, remember a woman so badly beaten and scarred who had *faith* in a baby, Baby Jesus, to change her entire life. Joy left with me a reminder of the best gift we all have been given, not a gift that was wrapped with a beautiful bow but a gift wrapped in a blanket that has changed all of our lives forever. *Joy to you* this season.

Joy from us,
Charles and Libby

Update from Libby

I could not believe my eyes when Joy showed up at our home. I had thought about her so much. And once again she had captured my word for the year, "faith." She actually said she was happy and she and the children were in church, even on Wednesday nights. She had a full-time job with the florist, and her favorite job was getting to put together the flower arrangements for several churches. She said her children would make fun of her when she wrote a note to their teachers or anyone. She signed her notes, "Joy, from Joy." She said all she hears in her head when she gets a little scared is "Jesus, others, you." Yes, she truly found her "faith."

Mugged at Christmas
(Christmas 2010)

When God gave us the gift of His Son, He gave us the fullest measure of all He could give. When Jesus' love fills our hearts, our hearts will always be full, no matter how much we give!

Give, and it will be given to you: good measure, pressed down, shaken together, and running over will be put into your bosom.
Luke 6:38

Devotional Thought

~ Roy Lessin

Construction has finally been completed at The Daltons (*for now anyway*).

Each group of workers who showed up became my "new best friends."

When each group left, I felt sad. Even though I had to be up early and dressed every morning, I was always glad to see them show up.

Every day became a day of excitement as I watched their progress. Every day was a day of excitement as I decided what snack I would surprise them with when break time arrived. I would remind them that their snack was on a little table that I had placed outside, and I would use my very best dishes to serve them. I spent hours looking for napkins that I could leave for them with special messages. My favorite napkins were "As for me and my house, we will serve the Lord" (Joshua 24:15). Each day as they came to their table, I watched from the window as they read their napkins before they ate.

One worker placed his napkin in his pocket every day, and I always wondered why. As they ate, this was my opportunity to pray for them and their safety while they worked at our home. When they had completed their task and left, I felt a little sad.

Then, the last crew arrived to work on our driveways and to expose red clay to not only us but to the entire neighborhood. Even in that, God was so gracious giving us neighbors who were also taking pride in what we were doing.

The workers in our last group were all big coffee drinkers. Now, this was fun for me because I am a Starbucks girl. Each day I prepared different coffees with whipped cream, cinnamon, chocolate, and anything my imagination could think of. I was also able to find coffee mugs with wonderful verses. My favorite verse was "I know the plans I have for you" (Jeremiah 29:11). I also watched as they lifted their mugs from the silver tray and read their verses. I, too, prayed a prayer each day for them for safety and their dependability.

They left, job completed, and I rejoiced and felt sad too that my mission was complete.

Then, right at Thanksgiving, the one worker I would have thought I would have never seen again appeared at the front door with a Christmas coffee mug for me. There was a Christmas message written on the mug. Could I hold back the tears? Yes, the tears flowed, and I thanked him from the bottom of my heart. He told me he would never forget us. I thanked him one more time before he left and told him I would never forget him. Oh, the verse, "I bring good news of great joy that will be for all people, a savior has been born to you; he is Christ the Lord" (Luke 2:10–11).

This Christmas, wherever you go, whatever you do, may the *joy* of Christmas find you,

Charles and Libby

Oh, would you think of "mugging" someone this Christmas?

Update from Libby

Boy, did this idea take off. I received so many calls and notes with friends telling me they had spent hours picking out just the right mug to give to someone special in their lives. And the napkins, I found several that Christmas with Jesus is the "reason for the season." At restaurants I would leave on the table packages of napkins with my ticket. I would hurry off for fear someone would chase me down to return them, thinking I had left them by accident. I prayed that they did not get thrown away. I received my answer when in one restaurant I returned to during the holidays, the waitress came over to the table and said she knew I had left them for her. She thanked me and said she did not know who had told me about her situation but as a child she had known the reason for Christmas but just had forgotten. She said from that day she realized Jesus still loved her with all her scars. I had no idea of her situation, but I do know the napkins did their job, along with Jesus.

Who will you "mug" this Christmas?

- ○ ....
- ○ ....
- ○ ....
- ○ ....
- ○ ....
- ○ ....
- ○ ....
- ○ ....
- ○ ....
- ○ ....
- ○ ....
- ○ ....
- ○ ....

Christmas Is a Piece of Cake
(Christmas 2011)

Jesus is:
The Fountain that quenches our thirst,
The Bread that nourishes our souls,
The Light that dispels our darkness,
The Physician that heals our wounds,
The Shepherd that guides our way into all that is good.

What a heart! What a love! What a Savior!

His name shall be called wonderful!
Isaiah 9:6

Devotional Thought

~ Roy Lessin

Bible study over, I headed to Fresh Market as I did every Tuesday. I pulled into the parking lot, reached for my purse, and spotted my one piece of chocolate pound cake that I had saved for myself. (*I had baked a cake for the ladies at Bible study and decided to save my slice to have with my afternoon coffee when I arrived home.*)

Shopping completed, I returned to my car, which I had left unlocked, loaded my groceries, jumped in, threw my purse into the seat, and immediately realized my cake was gone. How could that be? Must have fallen off the seat. No, not on the floor. Now, who would steal a piece of cake? I looked around the parking lot and saw nothing strange, and then I spotted a woman sitting on the curb. I walked over, told her what had happened, and ask her if she had noticed anyone around my car. She would not look at me, and she only said, "No." Aha, chocolate crumbs on the ground. What kept me from getting mad right at that moment? I truly do not know. I smiled, left, and headed home. I could not stop thinking about this woman.

The following Tuesday, I followed the same pattern except that I took lemon cake with me and left it on the seat. She also followed the same pattern because when I came out of the grocery store, my cake was gone. There she was. I walked over and spoke to her (*did not mention the cake*), and once again she had nothing to say.

I followed the pattern for five weeks and each week getting braver with what I placed in my seat. The sixth week, I came out of the store with two waters and preceded to give her one as I sat down next to her. She immediately took the water. (*I would too if I had just eaten a peanut butter and jelly sandwich that someone had left on their car seat for me.*) She finally began to talk. I guess she was so tired of listening to me each week.

I ask her where she lived, and she told me Travelers Rest. I ask if she had family, and she said "No" and got up and left immediately. *Ouch, that hurt.* I felt I would never see her again.

The next Tuesday, I returned with another lunch in my car. *Lord, please let her be there.* I did not see her when I went in, but when I came out, there she was in our same spot.

I told her I was sorry for asking questions, and I told her I had prayed all week that she would be at the store in our regular meeting place. "Why would you pray for me? You don't even know me." "I know you are a hurting child of God, and God has put me in charge of helping with the hurt." (*I know she thought "Is this woman crazy or what?"*)

It took several more weeks before she opened up (*several more lunches*). Finally, she told me that her daughter was killed in a car accident by someone texting, hitting her 17-year-old daughter's car, head on. After the funeral, she locked her house up, got in her car, and had lived there since December 15, 2009. Her brother was taking care of her house, but she could not go back home. Her husband had died Christmas 2008 with cancer. All she had was her daughter. Tears were flowing from both of us. We talked for another hour, and I left, saying, "I *will* see you next week."

I was so burdened when I left. My chest felt so heavy I did not know what to do. And then, God gave me the answer. I began to prepare for the following week.

The following week, after we had lunch together in the parking lot, I gave her all of my Christmas letters that I had written in the past years. I left them with her to read and said, "See you next week."

The following week, she talked a lot about her husband and daughter. It was different than the other times. I left with my same message, "See you next week." I had a feeling things were changing.

The following week, I prepared differently. When I arrived, I saw her immediately. I walked over to our spot, pulled out a Christmas cloth, a small Christmas tree, Christmas plates, and Christmas napkins. Two women sat there celebrating Baby Jesus with lunch and a whole chocolate pound cake with candles. I shared with her that only God could take away the pain and that Christmas was truly about the birth of Jesus. I reminded her that Jesus loved her, her husband, and her daughter.

She shared with me that it was time to go home. I knew in my heart she was right. She ask if she could take the tree home. "Of course," I said. She left me that day with me sitting on the curb. The last thing she shared was that she had not given me their real names. Her husband was *Jacob*, her daughter was *Grace*, and her name is… *Joy*.

May the newborn Jesus find a home in you this Christmas,
Charles and Libby
Luke 2:11

Update from Libby

When I found that my friend's true name was Joy, I could not believe it. I had to ask God why this word kept showing up in my life. Then, it all came together that God was sending me affirmations that "He" was present in everything I was doing and He alone made all of this happen. It was never about me. When Joy and I parted that last time, I felt a real loss. I cried all the way home. He never promised me that the Cross would not be heavy. Oh, the Christmas tree that I gave her was one that I had purchased for my mother many years ago, and when she passed away, I brought the sweet tree to our home. I tried to explain to God why I should not give it away. But I guess God and my mother had another idea.

Grandmother Fowler's Chocolate Pound Cake

2	sticks of butter
1/2	cup shortening
3	cups plain flour or cake flour
3	cups sugar
5	large eggs
1/2	teaspoon salt
1/2	teaspoon baking powder
1/2	cocoa sifted
1	teaspoon vanilla
1	cup milk

1. Cream butter, shortening, sugar, and eggs one at a time.
2. Add dry ingredients and milk alternately, and add vanilla.
3. Pour mixture in a greased and floured pound cake pan.
4. Bake at 325F oven for 1 hour and 15 minutes.

Miracle Moments
(Christmas 2012)

The gift of Jesus gives each person a reason to get up every morning with a joyful heart, to face the day in the freedom of forgiveness, and to walk with hope, carrying the promises of a faithful God into every tomorrow.

Thanks be to God for His indescribable gift!
II Corinthians 9:15 (NIV)

Devotional Thought

~ Roy Lessin

Missed my turn. Should have turned at that light. The next place I can turn is right here, no light, so much traffic. "Bam." What was that? I looked up in my mirror and watched as the car was spinning around in the road. I felt my heart in my throat. That was the light where I was. That would have been me, turning left. Traffic opened up, and I felt this urge to turn around and go back. As I returned to the accident, I felt the urge to get close and see if I could help. As I approached the car, I saw people trying to talk to the woman telling her help was on the way. I felt sick at my stomach when I realized who it was. It was Joy. Flashing through my brain, Fresh Market, having lunch, talking, crying with my friend, and now, here she was—she took my place. As I regained my thoughts, I pushed my way to the car (*I can be pushy at times*). I began to call her name, and she smiled as she realized it was me. All I could say was, "I am so sorry." This should have been me. She said, "You were right in front of me. I saw you but did not want to blow the horn. I know your car." She was right about that. I was reminded of all the times food and water were left on the front seat for her.

The ambulance arrived, and I told her I would follow them to the hospital. As I started to the hospital, my brain began to work (*second story*). Hold your thoughts.

I was at TJ Maxx shopping for a casserole dish. I happen to see this cute orange and white dress, threw it in my buggy, and kept moving. I was back in housewares, and this woman comes up and says, "I was just getting ready to buy that dress." I thought she must have the wrong dress. We were not exactly the same size. "I know there were several other dresses over there," I told her. "*Not* in the orange and white," she said. She then stormed off. Well, she was not going to rob me of my *joy*, and I knew she was confused because the dress just would not work for her.

I headed to the front of the store to pay for my treasures, and I was standing in line, so was the woman who was certainly not a happy camper. As I walked past her to walk up to the register, she called me a not nice name. I ignored her, but everyone heard and my face was very red.

I left the store, and as I got outside, I knew what I had to do. I waited, I took the dress out of the bag, and as she approached the place where I was standing, I stopped her, told her I wanted her to have the dress, and I was sorry all of this had happened. She grabbed the dress from my hand, and as she did, she began to cry, "Everyone hates me. My children hate me, my brother and sister hate me, my friends hate me," she said through her tears. Well, I didn't hate her, she was not my favorite person, but "hate" is a strong word. I ask if she wanted to go have a cup of coffee, so we headed to Barnes & Noble. Over coffee, she told me her husband had died of brain cancer. He only lived five months after he was diagnosed. It had been four months since he had died, and she was no better as she said. After a two-hour conversation, she was no longer the person I had encountered in the store. God has placed me in a unique place to continue to help a person facing such much hopelessness. From that day, Margaret and I talk and visit regularly.

Now, back to my original story. As I began to head to the hospital, I thought of Margaret. Joy had lost her husband to brain cancer, so had Margaret. Joy had even more grief with the loss of a daughter. I called Margaret and ask her if she could meet me at the Emergency Room. I was alright, but she was needed. She said she was on her way.

After eight hours at the hospital, Joy was allowed to go home with Margaret taking her. They have since become dear friends. Oh, Margaret called after she got Joy home to tell me she was settled in, but she said there was a little strangeness there. She said when she went in, Joy had a Christmas tree in the middle of her table. She said Joy told her to ask me about that.

Joy has always said that I saved her life. I have reminded her over and over that we know who saved her life. Joy also saved my life in many ways and not just from the wreck. Her story has allowed me to share with so many of you just who is responsible for all of us. Jesus showed up as a baby giving us something to rejoice about each and every day. Christmas: Our Savior brings a reminder of miracles that are around us each and every day. The biggest miracle we get to celebrate is Jesus. I know two new friends who are celebrating this year. Celebrate with them.

Blessed Christmas and Joy,
Charles and Libby

Update from Libby

"Miracle" is the only word I can use. Joy said I saved her life, but I believe she saved mine, in so many ways. Then, God allowed me to introduce Joy and Margaret who had so much in common, both losing their husbands to brain cancer. Now, the rest of this miracle. In 2015, Margaret began dating Joy's brother. Guess who got married in 2017? Nothing like watching God at work!

A Tisket, a Tasket, It's Just an Old Basket
(Christmas 2013)

Jesus came to make all things new within us. New life. New purpose. New desires. New heart. He does it all by His transforming love.

If anyone is in Christ, he is a new creation; old things have passed away; behold all things have become new.
2 Corinthians 5:17

Devotional Thought

~ Roy Lessin

I was driving to exercise, down one of the most beautiful streets in Greenville, thanking God for such a beautiful drive, and then I spotted it. It was trash day, and sitting on top of a trash can was an old basket. Surely, someone was not throwing the basket away. But it was on top of the trash can. I began to back up. With no one around, I removed the basket from its spot. (*Okay, I did not steal it because it was being thrown away.*) I placed the basket in my front seat, all the time wondering how it would look cleaned up and, wow, was it old.

I brought the basket home, placed it in the closet, and forgot about it for a few weeks. I had forgotten about the basket until I was getting some things out of the closet, and there it was. I immediately brought it to the kitchen and began to clean it up. What a beautiful basket, so old but so lovely.

My idea arrived. I began that day purchasing items to go in the basket—what wonderful treasures: napkins with scripture verses, a coffee mug with Charles' favorite verse (*Isaiah 40:31*), and several baked items. I placed a beautiful bow on the basket, and I was ready to go. I left for exercise the following morning with my basket. I knew because I go early, I was "safe." As I approached the house where I had borrowed the basket, I looked around for walkers, and seeing no one, I stopped, ran to the front door with the basket in my arms, placed it by the door, and took off. Afraid to look back, I preceded to drive onto exercise with my tummy feeling pretty happy.

About two months later, I came home one afternoon and spotted something sitting on our front porch.

It was the empty basket with a note that said, "Thank you for bringing something old back to life." Several weeks passed and I was traveling that same street. There was a young mother out front, and she flagged me down. She recognized my car and ask if I was the one who had brought the basket for her grandmother. I told her I was. She said her grandmother had passed away. She was staying at her grandmother's the morning I dropped the basket off and a neighbor knew my car, so that was how she found me. I ask if I could return the basket, and she said "No." It brought such *joy* that I needed to keep it.

I cannot keep this basket. All I can hear in my head is, *He can make all things new (Rev. 21:5)*. It is the season for giving. I had gotten the granddaughter's address because I had a book I told her I would send her. So, here I go, decorating the basket for Christmas. Again, Christmas napkins, Christmas mug, and all sorts of items and off to the post office to mail the basket. I sent a note asking Elizabeth not to return the basket. It belongs to her now, and I hope she will use it and think of her grandmother. For a few months, we did bring something old back to life. This Christmas season, remember someone *you* might have forgotten. Polish up something that has a meaning in your family. Or, polish yourself up for someone who might be thrilled to hear from you. Seek forgiveness, and seek the baby who makes this season so important for each of us.

Oh, I have to tell you, Elizabeth was the one who threw the basket away!

Merry Christmas and joy and blessings to each of you,
Charles and Libby

Update from Libby

Oh my gosh, after this letter went out, I heard so many wonderful stories from friends who had old baskets that they had decided to clean up, fill them with Christmas items, and give them to special people in their lives. They also ask if they could share my Christmas letter, and, of course, I was thrilled. I also told them I had a book I would love for them to put with their baskets: "Because of Jesus, Today Is Your Best Day." I still am not sure if that beautiful old basket got cleaned up or I did. I did hear from Elizabeth several years ago telling me she was still using the basket and she had placed old handkerchiefs of her grandmother in it. Oh, I just love old handkerchiefs. I have a collection from my grandmothers and mother. I did send one to Elizabeth to add to the collection. Guess that is why I feel God cleaned me up because I have never been able to part with my handkerchiefs.

Do you have a basket you can fill with treasures for someone this Christmas?

Be sure and list who the basket is for and your items.

- ○ ....
- ○ ....
- ○ ....
- ○ ....
- ○ ....
- ○ ....
- ○ ....
- ○ ....
- ○ ....
- ○ ....
- ○ ....

God's Appointments
(Christmas 2014)

Jesus is the good news of Christmas! He is the heart of love and all it gives, the heart of mercy and all it restores, the heart of kindness and all it embraces, and the heart of grace and all it provides.

I have come that they may have life,
and that they may have it more abundantly.
John 10:10

Devotional Thought

~ Roy Lessin

I truly *hope* each of you can follow my Christmas letter this year. Even I cannot believe how God worked this one out!

March 19, I jumped out of bed, headed to exercise, had a few extra minutes, and decided to look for some of my old journals. I was getting ready to start teaching a journaling class at the Dream Center and thought just maybe some of my old journals might help. Well, the first one I grabbed, I could not believe it. It fell open to my writing about attending the Anne Graham Lotz Revival that took place in Greenville in 2012. I had been involved with raising the money to bring her to Greenville. No one believed it could be done, but God knew which women to choose for this awesome task. Yes, Billy Graham's daughter showed up, and the Bi-Lo Center was completely full that Friday evening.

I was going to usher that evening. There was a young man whom I had prayed for several years, and that particular Friday, God placed it upon my heart to call him and just ask him to come. He knew about it because I had shared it with him on more than one occasion (*I can be pretty persistent at times*). I told him I would be ushering and in which section. The service began, and I sat down and left a seat on the end, just in case. In about five minutes, he showed up. What an incredible message that evening and at the end (*I was praying so hard*), she said, "I *never* do an extra verse, but tonight I feel it is necessary."

As the verse began, he said, "Miss D, I am ready." My legs could hardly get up. We were in the balcony, and with this young man's arms wrapped around my neck, we made our way to the front. Everyone stood up clapping and crying, and those that knew how long I had prayed for this young man, and all of my prayer warriors who had also prayed, rejoiced with us. That was March 19, 2012. Now, as I wept as I read this, I realized that here I was reading this, and it was March 19,

2014. Somehow, God had taken me to that same day two years later. I could not believe it.

Please hold that thought. The rest of this occurred the same day: March 19, 2014.

At least three times a week, God provides a drive for me down some of the most beautiful streets I have ever seen. In January, I had just turned left on one of these streets, and as I drove, I had this unbelievable sensation to begin praying for someone on that street. I looked around and saw no one. With my heart pounding, I actually felt sick. I began praying for this person and prayed that God would reveal to them that God had placed someone in their path to pray for them. I continued on my drive, and for several months, I prayed this same prayer every time I drove down this street.

Now, on March 19, 2014, I was having coffee with a dear friend, and I had taken my 2012 journal with me to show her and tell her what had happened that morning and read to her what I had written on that day, exactly two years ago. We shared a God-filled morning, staying longer and sharing longer than we ever had.

I left and realized I had left my journal on the table. I panicked. I headed back and ran in, and there was my journal, on the table, in the hands of a young woman who was very embarrassed she was reading it. It was open to March 19, 2012. Okay, this was definitely God's appointment. I sat down, we talked, and we made the decision to meet again in a week. We met on three occasions before I realized what was happening. She finally said, "I live really close to here." She told me the street, and she saw the shock on my face. I told her I had been praying for her at least three times a week as I drove down her street. She then told me that when we met the first time, she had made the decision to kill herself and was trying to figure out the best way. We talked on, and she told me her story and I told her what I could do to help. No, what God could do through me to help her.

To try and write anymore, I cannot. To know each day that God has appointments for each of you, I *know* He does! The most important appointment we can all share is the appointment that God shared with each of us, the birth of *Jesus*, one that I am so thankful I did not miss and so glad none of you missed it either.

Joy!

Charles and Libby

Update from Libby

What a great feeling to see someone accept Jesus as their Savior. Years of prayers, on my knees, and once again in God's timing. God carried both of us down that aisle that night. March 19, another soul added to Heaven.

Then we fast-forward to a young mother who picked my journal up, and it fell open to March 19. How embarrassed she was when I walked up. I had the strangest feeling when I saw her and once again knew it was one of those God nudges. For all the struggles she experienced, she is now doing so great. She believes in God's appointments now, and she says one appointment she always keeps is March 19 when she spends her day with God. Divine appointments—yes both of these were "divine appointments." March 19, still sometimes I have to stop and say, "How can anyone not believe in God?"

Have a Blessed Day
(Christmas 2015)

When God gave us the gift of His Son, no spiritual blessing was withheld from us. And from those blessings come boundless opportunities for us to bless others.

Out of His fullness we all received one grace after another and spiritual blessing upon spiritual blessing.
John 1:16 (Amplified)

Devotional Thought

~ Roy Lessin

We were in Scottsdale, Arizona. Charles was at the car show, and I was going to do a little shopping.

I drove to the mall, parked the car, and headed in, but not before I noticed a woman getting food out of the trash can right beside the door. I pretended not to see her. She did the same.

I shopped for a few hours, but my heart was not in it. All I could think about was the woman. I decided that maybe my day would get better if I stopped for lunch. I went into a restaurant that had just opened that had Chinese food. It really looked great. Only one problem, the guy spoke no English, and I kept telling him all I wanted was the orange chicken and no sides. He kept insisting that I had to take two sides. Okay, I finally gave in and chose the sides, and just as I did, it hit me. Lord, thank you for making me purchase all three. I told him to carry out a bottle of water, a cup, and two forks. I left, heading to the direction where I came in. Same nervous stomach every time God does this to me. I didn't wonder if she would be there—I knew she would be.

Yes, she was there, sitting on a bench as if she were waiting on me. I sat down and began my nervous chatter, asking her to share my lunch. I told her I did not know anyone there and that I hated eating by myself. She immediately said, "Okay." She was so hungry. This was one time I did not have to ask a lot of questions. She began by saying her husband had moved them there from Texas and then he told her he was leaving and he packed up and left and she and the children had been on their own for about five weeks. She had enough money for one more month of rent, and that was it. She was so scared. Going back home was a worse option. She was looking for a job, but so far, nothing. She said she had been feeding the children from the dumpster behind the mall. She was afraid to tell the school because she did not want them to take her children. I ask her where she had worked in the past, and she said at a drug store and a grocery store.

Well, I ask her if she would pray with me, and she said, "Yes," and I prayed thanking God for her new job. I had been to the CVS that was right there at the mall earlier that week, so I told her we would go there and put in an application. Off we went, me praying the entire time. The store manager was there, and I introduced him to "my friend" (*well she was by now*) who needed a job really bad and ask if they had any openings. They had an opening for 4:00–12:00. He allowed us to put in an application, and I told him that I felt sure he was just about to hire the best employee he would ever have. He said, "Okay. If she passes the drug test, I will give her a try." References, he never ask, but she did put me down as one, and I listed Charles as another. (*I knew Charles wouldn't care, but I don't think I told him immediately I had done that.*)

She got the job! She started a week later and had a neighbor who was a widow who needed extra money, and she slept over with the children. Now, does God provide or what?

As I began my Christmas letter, I called and checked on Maria. She is now working the 9:00–5:00 schedule, and she says her boss says I was right—she is the best employee he has ever had. She promised me she would pray with the children every day and take them to church. She has kept that promise. She also said her boss finally told her why he hired her. He said he was at the register when I came in before, and he heard me tell the girl on the register, "Have a blessed day." He said after that, he was afraid not to give her a try.

God has blessed all of us so much, and this time of year, He blessed us with the greatest gift ever, *His Son*. Please, *bless* someone today. My blessings overflow, and one of my biggest blessings is all of *you*!

Charles and Libby

Update from Libby

In 2016, when we arrived in Scottsdale, Arizona, I went straight to the CVS and was told Maria no longer worked there. I ask to speak to the manager to find out what had happened. Oh my gosh, he was so excited to tell me she had been moved to another store. She was also being trained to become an assistant manager. He said she never failed to tell people how much she loved Jesus. Through one of her husband's friends, she was able to locate her husband. After two years, he returned to her and the children. She told him he would have to go to church with them. He is now custodian at the church. God is always available and never silent.

Blue Light Special
(Christmas 2016)

There is an eternal smile upon the heart that has been forgiven and received the gift of eternal life.

As many as received Him (Jesus), to them He gave the right to become children of God, to those who believe in His name.
John 1:12

Devotional Thought

~ Roy Lessin

He pulled out of the side street, right behind me. I knew I was not speeding. Well, I didn't think I was. I did become a little concerned when he turned on our street and into our driveway right behind me (*no blue light turned on, and hopefully none of our neighbors were at home*).

I immediately jumped out of the car, asking that if he didn't mind, I could please go inside and put my ice cream in the freezer, and I would come right back out. With a shocked expression, he said "Yes." I ran into the house and right back out. In my nervous chatter, I began if I was speeding, and I didn't think I was; I was hurrying to get home with my ice cream. It was so hot and the air in my car was messed up, and as expensive as Breyers ice cream is, I didn't want it to melt. Before I could say anything else, he put his hand up to stop me, and then he began to laugh. He could not stop. I became embarrassed thinking, *now he thinks, what a strange woman.* I noticed as he laughed, his laughter turned into tears and the next thing I knew I was asking if he was alright, and he began his story. He said it was a long time since he felt any laughter. His mom had passed away five months ago, and their final words were not good, and he had been in a state of depression ever since. I sensed he was becoming worried about himself.

"Was your mom concerned about your salvation?" Where did that come from? I felt that God nudge once again. "Yes," he said, "and how did you know? I just wasn't ready," he said. "Hey, God can fix that today," I said. "You just pulled into the right driveway (*forgetting about my ticket*). I personally know Jesus. He lives in our home, and I would say you were sent here today. I could feel my heart beating so fast, I almost lost my breath."

We talked and by the time we had finished talking in our driveway, we prayed together, and he asked Jesus into his heart. I went inside to get him some peach tea (*what a hot day*) and thought maybe I will just give him some copies of past Christmas letters.

I went back outside, gave him the letters, and explained that maybe after reading a few of my letters, he would see that God's timing is always right.

Just as Jesus sent his precious Son to be born in a manager, he also found another one of his children who needed him. Baby Jesus' birth was for me and my new friend. This Christmas will have a new meaning for one more and for a mother whose prayers have been answered just as Mary's prayers were answered for her son.

(*By the way, no ticket. He was trying to tell me I had a taillight burned out*).

Yes, God works in mysterious ways, even with a baby whose birth we celebrate this Christmas.

A very Merry Christmas,
Charles and Libby

Update from Libby

When the officer pulled out of our driveway, all I could do was pray, "God, you take it from here." I did not see him again until two years later. He shared how happy he was and that he had a girlfriend and she loved Jesus like I did. She told him Jesus lived in her apartment, and he told her he was not sure about that because he had met a lady that told him Jesus lived in her home. We both left laughing, quite different from our first meeting. I am so glad God speaks to each of us just right where we are.

Please take some time to Be Still. Can you hear God speaking to you?

ABIDE IN JESUS AND HE WILL ABIDE IN YOU.

FULL CIRCLE, GOD'S CIRCLE
(CHRISTMAS 2017)

Despite the power of the Roman Empire to defeat God's plan and the resistance of the Scribes and Pharisees to cancel God's plan, God's redemptive plan was fulfilled in every detail through His Son, the Lord Jesus Christ. God is always working out His plan.

I indeed have spoken it; I will also bring it to pass.
I have purposed it; I will also do it.
Isaiah: 46:11

Devotional Thought

~ Roy Lessin

In 2015, I had an experience that I was never sure I would write about until I saw this year just how amazing God is.

My friend was leaving to return to Germany, and we were meeting her husband at Costco for them to head to the airport. After shopping, she borrowed my phone, called her husband, and told him what time to be at Costco. We met her husband out front, and they said a very tearful goodbye, and we parted, me heading to my car and them driving away. I reached for my phone and realized my phone was headed to Germany. It was in my friend's bag, not mine. In a panic, I jumped in my car, heading for home to see if I had written down her husband's cell phone. Just as I got to the QT Station, it hit me. If I could borrow a phone, I could call my phone and she would hear it ring, and all would be alright. As I pulled in, there was a man sitting out front, with his Harley parked there and all dressed to ride. I quickly explained my problem, asking if I could borrow his phone. His comment was, "Okay, but if my wife sees this call, you might have to explain to her why you borrowed my phone." "Of course," I told him. I called three times, no answer. I quickly said, "Thank you," and hollered over my shoulder, "Have a blessed day." I jumped in my car and drove home. By the time I arrived, my friend had left a message at our home to say she realized she had my phone and they were driving to our house. (*Thank you Lord*).

The next day I was driving to an Fellowship of Christian Athletics board meeting, and my phone rang, but no one was there. I hung up, and it rang again. He began by saying he was the man at the QT Station the day before. He was crying, and he began to tell me his story. He and his wife were separating, and he did not want this to happen. He had taken the day off from work, and he was going to drive to the mountains, drive his Harley off the road, and kill himself. By then, I had pulled over, feeling sick. He then said when I said, "Have a blessed day," he realized he was not supposed to do this. He decided to call his wife. They had talked most of the night, and they both agreed they needed to get help. There is so much more to this story, but the most important message is they are back together and in church together, and he tells everyone about this angel, who was dressed in white and even driving a white car who God sent just for him. (*Okay, Charles says he was really confused*).

In the remainder of this story, you will have to remember back to last year about the policeman who followed me home and found Jesus in our driveway. His story continues.

I was pumping gas (*what is this with gas stations*), and this policeman walked up behind me and ask if he could pump my gas. Well, yes, it was the same policeman, and he said he had been by the house several times, trying to catch me at home. He told me he had joined a wonderful church and was going regularly. Then he said that the first of this year, he decided to share his story in his Sunday school class about the person who had led him to Jesus. He also shared that as he left her home, she said, "Have a blessed day." He said, when he finished, one of the men in his Sunday school class began asking questions and asked him to describe the woman's car. When he did, he said the man began to sob and told his story about this woman who saved his life at the QT Station. He realized they were talking about the same person when the policeman said the woman said to him, "Have a blessed day." Well, by then we were both crying, and I was in shock. I honestly could not take it all in. We talked for a while longer, and as we both left in tears, he shouted to me, "Have a blessed day!" Gosh, I was already blessed, and I pray this will bless you in the way it has blessed me.

God is working all the time. Allow God to complete the circle for you this Christmas by surrounding yourselves with those you love.

Charles and I send our love to each of you,
Charles and Libby

Decide TODAY to just say, "Have a Blessed Day."

You will feel a blessing and JOY. It gets easier and easier.

Update from Libby

After this sweet couple got back together, I had an opportunity to meet his wife. We met early one morning at the same station, and I took my silver tea set, coffee mugs, and napkins with scriptures. I placed all of this on the table outside of the station. I went in, got us coffee and pastries, and returned to spend an hour just listening. (Several people took pictures.) Each day God speaks to us. That day I stopped at the station, God spoke to this desperate man just from me saying, "Have a blessed day." And if I had not used his phone, he would have never had my phone number. Maybe you can say to someone, "Have a blessed day," and see what happens.

The remainder of this story of how God placed the policeman in the same Sunday school class with this couple is a true miracle. God is a connector. Just with four words, "Have a blessed day," God was able to deliver a powerful message. Sometimes he calls on us to share in His purpose. Other times, He just speaks softly and reminds us of His amazing love for us.

I have the Joy, Joy, Joy, Joy Down in My Heart

(Christmas 2018)

Why did heaven's angels appear one night to lowly shepherds on a lonely hillside? When God revealed His plan to the shepherds, they listened in wonder, obeyed with promptness, and shared what they discovered with zeal and joy.

I bring you good tidings of great joy which shall be to all people.
For there is born to you this day in the city of David a Savior,
who is Christ the Lord.
Luke 2:10, 11

Devotional Thought

~ Roy Lessin

For some reason I have been asked many times this year, "When did you feel that first God nudge?" I would reply each time, "I honestly do not remember." Then all of a sudden, early one morning, I did remember.

I was in the seventh grade and the adult choir at our church invited our middle school choir to sing in the Christmas cantata with them. I was so excited, and above all of that, I was given a solo.

There is just one problem with all of this: we had one girl in our choir who was tone deaf. She had no idea how bad she sounded, and she loved to sing. No one wanted to stand by her, so I volunteered to have her next to me. I could tune out anybody (*so my mother always said*).

As we began to practice, practices were really bad. Then my first idea came. Plan A: The adult choir director also taught voice lessons. I took lessons from him and loved it. I knew my friend could not afford lessons, so I ask my parents if I could cut my hour lesson to 30 minutes and she could have the other 30 minutes. They agreed, as I knew they would, and my voice teacher agreed. I explained to my friend that I just could not do but 30 minutes, and he was charging me for an hour. Would she go the other 30 minutes? She showed up early every week. As she practiced, I would sit outside and listen. At first, it hurt my ears, and as time went on, she honestly improved (*I thought*).

Then, we began practice with the full choir. I could hear the difference in her voice. Plan B: I talked to my voice teacher about teaching her my solo. At first he said, "No!" And then, the more I begged, he agreed to try. They began and after several weeks, my teacher and I noticed a significant change in her voice. Plan C: "*Please* give her my solo," I begged. "I know she can do it. *Please!*" Finally, he agreed, and we also agreed to tell no one. He told her the following week, and she was so excited and then sad for me. Not me. I was very happy. Hey, I sang all the time.

The night of the cantata came, and we had to arrive at 5:00 pm for one final run-through. I sang my part during practice, and she smiled knowing what was going to take place later. Then, she came to me and said, "I cannot do it." I immediately said, "Yes you can. You have trained for this, you have to." Plan D: I ran around looking for a magic marker and found one but no paper. I immediately pulled off my slip and began to write.

Time for the cantata. As my part got closer, my heart beating so fast, I left the choir. I could feel the eyes and questions. I immediately ran around to the front of the church and opened the doors, and in full site of my friend, I held my slip up with the words written on it, "GOD LOVES YOU."

She saw me and stood up so straight. Our director began to direct her, and she sang perfectly. Oh, the faces in the choir, everyone who had made fun of her behind her back. Tears streamed down my face. We did it. Afterward, I went to my parents who were right on the front row where they always were when I sang. I felt I needed to explain, but in joyful tears, they understood already. I watched all of the people surrounding my friend and the joy in her parents' faces. I felt such *joy* like I have never felt before. God must have felt my kind of *joy* when baby Jesus was born.

Please, in this Christmas season, place *joy* in your heart, and share it with someone.

Charles and Libby

Update from Libby

About 30 years after this experience, we decided to visit another church in the area. When the choir came out, I could not believe my eyes. There was my friend from the seventh grade in the choir. I was so excited. As soon as the service was over, I made my way to the front of the church and just screamed her name out. She recognized me immediately. We hugged, and she told me they had just moved to our area, and the first thing they did was find a church, and she immediately joined the choir. We did not talk about what happened so many years ago, but as I got ready to walk off, she hugged me and said, "Thank you." If we know God, we can tell if what we feel led to do is from Him or not. At that early age, I felt his presence directing me.

What a Day
(Christmas 2019)

Jesus, Immanuel, came from heaven and became a man for a glorious purpose: our reconciliation! He came to bring us, who were separated from God, into fellowship with God. Jesus wants to take your hand and place it in the hand of your heavenly Father.

God has reconciled us to Himself through Jesus Christ…on Christ's behalf, be reconciled to God.
2 Corinthians 5:19, 20

Devotional Thought

~ Roy Lessin

What a day. I finally headed home and decided to go a different way. Who knows? I may found out pretty quick. I turned on Grove Road, and as I did, I noticed a young boy in the middle of the road waiting to cross. No median, Lordy, be careful. As I approached him, something in me said, *Go very slow*. Just as I approached him, he stepped right out in front of me. I heard the noise and saw him disappear, and I turned my wheels and slammed on my brakes. No car in the other lane, thank you, Lord. I jumped out of the car, and there he was just sitting in the road.

Screaming at him, I asked, "Are you alright? What in the world were you thinking? Did I hit you? Are you hurt?" Still no answer. By then several others had stopped. One guy said he did it on purpose and we needed to call the police. The child screamed "No!" He then stood up, said I did not hit him, and began to cry. Such an uproar around us of everyone saying he did it on purpose. Finally, as people settled down, I told the boy I needed to move my car out of the road or if I drove to the McDonalds on the corner, would he walk there and meet me and maybe get a coke or ice cream. The one really vocal guy said I was crazy, but at that point, my heart was beating so fast I could hardly catch my breath. The boy agreed, and I turned my car around, heading for McDonalds, not sure if he would show or not. I was shaking so bad and praying the entire time, *God, thank you this child is alright. God, I am not asking if I am doing the right thing. All I know is I feel I am listening to you.*

I walked into McDonalds and waited, and it honestly seemed like forever. (*No, I am not a patient person*). I was sitting there praying, and he walked up. My first words were, "I was praying you would come." He started crying, and my natural reaction was to get up and hug him. I held him close for what seemed like forever with everyone walking by looking at us. When he finally stopped, I got him something to drink and eat. I tried to stay calm, but I had to know just why he had done this. I tried to be kind but also told him just how dangerous that was. Finally, he told me his name was Michael, he was 10, and that he did not need to live. He had nobody to take care of him. Feeling sick at my stomach, I tried to find out where he lived and why there was no one for him. He said his grandma was over in the hospital and she was going to die. Why do you think that I ask? Cause she has cancer and it is bad. After much more conversation, I told him I would go back with him to see his grandmother. At first, he said, "No," and then he agreed after I told him I would not tell her what happen. We headed to the hospital, and he took me to her room. When we walked into the room, he screamed out, "Grandma!" There was a woman kneeling by the bed crying, and he thought his grandmother had gone to heaven. His grandmother was able to barely open her eyes. The woman by the bed stood up and saw Michael and I hand in hand, and boy did I feel out of place. I told her I had met Michael at McDonalds, and he wanted me to meet his grandmother. I ask if I could pray with them, and she said I have just told God, I honestly cannot pray. Why would God take my mother? She is so good.

After much conversation, she told me Michael's parents were both in jail. I told her that her mother was so tired, but she was giving her a gift of her grandson. The aunt was also alone, and she and Michael held each other tight. I had to leave; I felt like God was finished with me. I reminded them of the season we were going into, and just as God brought baby Jesus into the world, he had brought them. My last words were, "You two be a star for him. Shine for your mother and grandmother." I truly have no other words.

Be joyful this season,
Charles and Libby

Update from Libby

For several months, I could not travel the road where all of this happen. All I could think about was what if I had hit this child. Then finally, I decided to place myself on a journey that I needed to take. As I made that turn, I felt sick to my stomach and just had to pull over the first place I could. Of course my radio was on, and the song that started playing was a choir singing, "This little light of mine, I'm gonna let it shine." I began to let the tears flow, and I remembered my last words to Michael and his aunt were, "Be a star for him, and shine for your mother and grandmother."

Today Is Our Best Day
(Christmas 2020)

Is there a deeper love than God's love for you?
Is there a greater gift than God's salvation?
Is there a wiser decision than following Jesus?
Is there a richer treasure than the Lord's presence?
Is there a higher destination than Heaven's home?
Is there a surer hope than what God has prepared for those who love Him?
Is there?

For God so loved the world that He gave His only begotten Son, that whoever believes in Him should not perish but have everlasting life.
John 3:16

Devotional Thought

~ Roy Lessin

Watching the evening news, they told of a 33-year-old man who had served in the military and came home to South Carolina, and while working as a security guard, he had been shot and killed while he was protecting the establishment where he was employed. I could not get this off my mind. I even wrote his name down.

The next few days, I began to go through the obituaries, and I found this man's name. It gave his mother's address at the end. I kept feeling I needed to do something. After a week, I sat down, wrote his mother a note, and sent her a copy of the book my friend and I have given out to thousands of people, *Because of Jesus, Today Is Your Best Day*. I placed them in an envelope, prayed, and mailed them. I began to say, "Lord, I hope I heard you clearly." About two weeks later, I received a very warm note from the mother. My heart was so full of thanksgiving.

Fast-forward all the way to November. I was at the grocery store. I had just pulled in, had the top down on my car, and was listening to a beautiful song entitled "Eye of the Storm." Yes, I might have had my radio a little loud. I did not notice the woman sitting in the car next to me on the phone.

The woman got out of her car, caught my eye, and said, "I love that song. I think I have heard it." I immediately apologized that I had my radio turned so loud. All of a sudden, she noticed a copy of *Because of Jesus, Today Is Your Best Day* laying in my seat. She said, "Oh my gosh, I have that same book. I received a copy of it when my son died." I began to shake all over. All I could think to say is, "Do you have time to go back in the grocery store and let me treat you to a coffee?" (*This*

Starbucks girl can always drink a peppermint mocha.) She said she did, and later said she could not believe she did that.

Well, in our conversation, I had to hold my coffee with two hands because I was shaking so badly. I began to explain how I had had that God nudge, and I was the one who had sent the book to her. She began to weep, and somehow it just did not matter where we were. We were in a place that at that time only God could have brought us. She told me, "As you know, I do not live on this side of town. I was so down this morning and could not go into my normal grocery store where I always run into someone who wants to tell me they are grieving for me. I did not need that." She had heard how nice this store was and she needed a change of scenery. Well, she sure got it! We talked on, and she ask me again why her, why did I feel I should send her anything? I explained that only God could have done that. Only God could have placed her at the grocery store with me. We left after we prayed together. I left with a totally different feeling about the holidays. Yes, this year might look a little different, but hey, *nothing can rob us of our joy. Jesus is still the reason for the season.*

Merry Christmas and so much love,
Charles and Libby

Update from Libby

I almost did not listen to God when He told me to send this woman this powerful little book. I even doubted after I placed it in the mail. Then, that beautiful November day, once again, God showed up and showed out. As we talked over coffee, I was reminded how God can speak through each of us. She ended up ministering to me saying her son would want her to forgive this man who had taken her son's life. She said when she first received the book, she did not read it. Then, after a week, she picked it up, and as she started flipping through the book, the words caught her eyes: "GRACE makes it possible for today to be YOUR best day." That is when she realized that only God would have provided those words for her to see. Then she told me the reason she loved the song, "In the Eye of the Storm." One line says, "In the middle of the war, you guard my soul." She had forgotten she had listened to that song over and over when her son was in the military. After he was killed, God woke her up hearing those words. She said she knew then that once again God did remain in control. Those were the last words we exchanged. She ministered to me that day.

Trucking Along with Jesus
(Christmas 2021)

Look in the Manger

When others fail, hurt, or disappoint you,
look in the manger—the Wonderful One is there!

When you are perplexed, confused, or needing direction,
look in the manger—the Counselor is there!

When you lack strength or courage,
look in the manger—the Mighty God is there!

When demands and schedules bring stress and pressure,
look in the manger—the Prince of Peace is there!

When you are lost, empty, and afraid,
look in the manger—the Savior is there!

When you need to know you are loved with an everlasting love,
look in the manger—Jesus is there!

And the Shepherds went back, glorifying and praising God for all that they had heard and seen, just as had been told them.
Luke 2:20

Devotional Thought

~ Roy Lessin

It was a beautiful Monday morning, and I headed to Bible study and top down on my car, listening to some great Christian music. All of a sudden, I hear this horn blowing on this eighteen-wheeler truck next to me. I ignored it, not thinking he was blowing at me. As we moved along, he stayed right with me. He would barely blow his horn like he was trying to get my attention. Suddenly, I thought, *Something must be wrong with my car.* I looked up, and he pointed to the passenger side of my car, gave me a thumbs up, and then drove off.

When COVID-19 began, I had talked to my Bible study group with an idea: To help keep our spirits up and maybe the spirit of someone else, let's take a Bible, and place it on the passenger's seat, and maybe someone who may be getting in or out of their car would see it, and it just might give them *hope* and reassurance of who was truly in control. Well, that was what he saw: my red Bible lying in the seat. Who would have dreamed a trucker would spot my Bible. I did a high five as we both drove off (sorry, we slowed down traffic behind us). The seed was planted.

Now, seven months later, another Monday, in the same road, heading to Bible study, I pulled into the QT Station. Before pumping my gas, I pulled up front, ran inside to get me a passion fruit tea (which one of my sweet friends got me hooked on), came out the door, and drank my tea, and there was this man just leaning against my car. At first I thought, *What is he doing?* Then, all of a sudden, I had that strange feeling I was supposed to be nice to him. He said, "You don't remember me, do you?" I said, "No," and he said, "Who could forget this car?" He said, "So you still have your Bible on the front seat. That's my truck over there. I drive this route every Monday, and I saw your car when I pulled in for gas". Oh my gosh, my trucker! He asked me why I had a Bible on my seat all of the time. I told him about my Bible study group and how we placed a Bible on the seat to give just one person *hope* when they saw it. I told him it also made me feel like God was my copilot.

We began a long conversation about him and how he grew up in church, but he and his family were no longer active. He said he wasn't sure that God even knew he was still around. Wow, I assured him that God was as close to him today as he was when he was a child. Did he think it was an accident he saw my Bible? Was it an accident we pulled into the station together? I also had a copy of Roy Lessin's book *Because of Jesus Today Is Your Best Day* on my front seat. I told him my friend and I (and several others) have given out hundreds of these. "Please read one a day" is what I ask him to do. He was so open to hearing and talking about Jesus. That certainly made me happy. We agreed it was up to him to share our encounter with his family. He said very nervously that he would. I also told him to help keep God in his heart all the time that maybe every time he passes a QT, he would think of that as his *quiet time* with Jesus. He laughed and said that could be quite a few. "Just thank God, is all ya have to do" is what I told him. A simple prayer. I reminded him of the season we were approaching and why he had a reason to celebrate.

Will this Christmas be different for my trucker friend? I have to believe that it will. Because of baby Jesus, all of this began—because God chose to be real to him, he has done the same for us by sending us a baby who came to save the world. And he has added a trucker to the family this year. Please share Jesus and *hope* to someone this Christmas. Oh, one final note, I forgot to get my gas.

With *love* and *hope* this Christmas,
Charles and Libby

Update from Libby

I never run early for Bible study. This particular day I did, so I decided to stop at the QT and buy myself a passion fruit ice tea (unsweetened) to take with me to Bible study. As I began to get close to the QT Station, it hit me; I know why I am early. My new friend, the trucker, is going to be there. As I pulled in, I saw the large blue truck but no one in it. I hurried inside and didn't see him. As I left the store, there he was standing by my car smiling so big. I hurried toward him and, without thinking, gave him a big hug (he hugged me back). He began talking so fast I could hardly keep up. Our conversation ended with "He found out he had not forgotten how to pray." He ask me to walk to his truck with him, and there on the seat was a copy of the book I had given him. The book looked very worn. I went back to my car and got him an extra copy of the book and told him to look for an opportunity to share it with someone else. We both left there with joyful hearts. The next time I see him, I will give him a Bible to place on his seat. Yes, it will happen—God will plan it, not Libby.

Libby's Orange Cranberry Muffins

2	cups all-purpose flour
1	teaspoon baking powder
1/2	teaspoon baking soda
1/2	teaspoon salt
3/4	cups of sugar
1	cup cranberries (I usually use dried cranberries, but you can also use fresh ones.)
1	egg
1/4	cup vegetable oil
3/4	cup orange juice
1	tablespoon orange grated orange rind

1. Combine dry ingredients.
2. Stir in cranberries.

3. Beat egg, orange juice, oil, and orange rind together. Add to the mixture of dry ingredients.
4. Stir just enough to moisten (secrets to muffins: stir just enough to mix; there will be lumps, but do not worry).
5. Spoon into greased muffin cups (I also use muffin baking cups), and fill 3/4 full (this will make 12 muffins, but I like to make jumbo muffins also, so you can just make 6 large muffins).
6. Sprinkle the tops with a little bit of sugar.
7. Bake at 400F for 15–20 minutes. They will be nice and brown. Enjoy!

About the Authors

Libby Dalton, a Southern girl, has enjoyed a career in banking, owning her own Dynamic Image business, hospital marketing, and public relations. She ended her professional career a few years ago as president and CEO of a local YMCA.

Libby is currently active in a women's Bible study and looks every day for ways to show someone Jesus. Her husband Charles says, "She sees what most of us walk right past!" During these super active years, she has maintained a real passion for cooking.

Libby resides in Greenville, South Carolina, and her life continues to be enriched by her husband, three children, two daughter-in-laws, and three grandchildren. The grandchildren will never forget their 13 years of attending *Grandma's Camp* during the July 4th week each of those summers.

Roy Lessin is an ordained minister of the gospel, a Bible teacher, and a former Christian education director, and he served the Lord with his wife, Charlene, in Mexico and Puerto Rico before becoming one of the four founders of DaySpring Cards in 1971. Roy's writing ministry has continued for over 50 years through cards, books, and online devotionals.

Back Cover

My heart just starts beating so fast. I can hardly breathe. I get my chill bumps (Jesus bumps). Then, I realize God has put me here for this time. I pray each morning, "God, open my eyes, and let me see what you have for me today. Please don't let me miss an opportunity to be there for someone else."

Each Christmas letter in this little book is a *gift* from God, an opportunity not missed. While everything we do emphasizes the pursuit of pleasure, success, and even wealth, let's pursue God's assignment for us instead. Look for the opportunities; *please* do not miss a single one. If they are there for me, they are there for you too.

You will enjoy the wisdom of Roy Lessin and his wonderful messages he shares with each story. How God brought us together is just another example of how BIG our God is.

My prayer for each of you is just like Christmas, "Ya gotta believe and pray."

Enjoy!

CPSIA information can be obtained
at www.ICGtesting.com
Printed in the USA
BVHW091108290922
648154BV00001B/1